I0541674

I Am Purpose

SECTION 1:

WHAT IS SPIRITUAL WELLNESS

PURPOSE & MEANING

And we know that all things work together for the good of those who love God, to those who are the call according to his purpose. - Romans 8:28

SECTION 1: CHAPTER 1
PURPOSE & MEANING

And we know that all things work together for the good of those who love God, to those who are the call according to his purpose. – Romans 8:28

And we know that all things work together for the good of those who love God, to those who are the call according to his purpose. - Romans 8:28

And we know that all things work together for the good of those who love God, to those who are the call according to his purpose. - Romans 8:28

And we know that all things work together for the good of those who love God, to those who are the call according to his purpose. - Romans 8:28

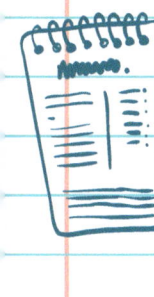

And we know that all things work together for the good of those who love God, to those who are the call according to his purpose. – Romans 8:28

Visions

Goals

Milestones

Habits

Spiritual Reflection

Personal Reflection

SEARCHING FOR ANSWERS TO BIG QUESTIONS

And you will seek me and find me, when you search for me with all your heart. – Jeremiah 29:13

SECTION 1: CHAPTER 2
SEARCHING FOR ANSWERS TO BIG QUESTIONS

And you will seek me and find me, when you search for me with all your heart. –

Jeremiah 29:13

And you will seek me and find me, when you search for me with all your heart. –

Jeremiah 29:13

And you will seek me and find me, when you search for me with all your heart. – Jeremiah 29:13

And you will seek me and find me, when you search for me with all your heart. – Jeremiah 29:13

And you will seek me and find me, when you search for me with all your heart. – Jeremiah 29:13

Visions

Goals

Milestones

Habits

Spiritual Reflection

Personal Reflection

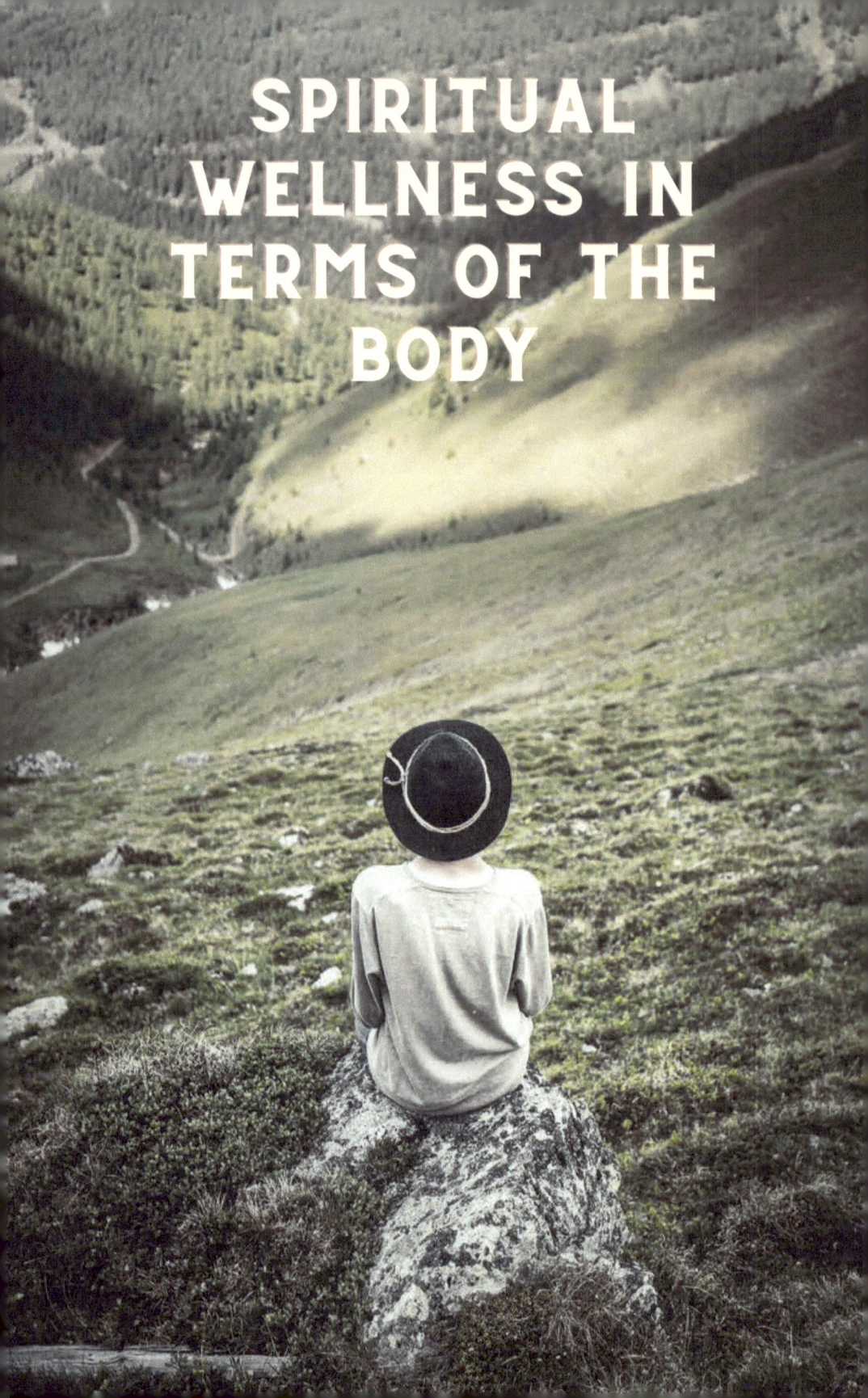

SPIRITUAL WELLNESS IN TERMS OF THE BODY

For as the body is one and has many members, but all the members of that one body, being many, are one body, so also is Christ. - I Corinthians 12

SECTION 1: CHAPTER 3
SPIRITUAL WELLNESS IN TERMS OF THE BODY

For as the body is one and has many members, but all the members of that one body, being many, are one body, so also is Christ. – I Corinthians 12

For as the body is one and has many members, but all the members of that one body, being many, are one body, so also is Christ. - I Corinthians 12

For as the body is one and has many members, but all the members of that one body,

being many, are one body, so also is Christ. - I Corinthians 12

For as the body is one and has many members, but all the members of that one body,

being many, are one body, so also is Christ. – I Corinthians 12

For as the body is one and has many members, but all the members of that one body, being many, are one body, so also is Christ. – I Corinthians 12

Visions

Goals

Milestones

Habits

Spiritual Reflection

Personal Reflection

SPIRITUAL WELLNESS IN TERMS OF THE MIND AND SOUL

"Thou wilt keep him in perfect peace, whose mind is stayed on thee; because he trusteth in thee." - Isaiah 26:3

SECTION 1: CHAPTER 4
SPIRITUAL WELLNESS IN TERMS OF THE MIND AND SOUL

"Thou wilt keep him in perfect peace, whose mind is stayed on thee; because he trusteth in thee." - Isaiah 26:3

"Thou wilt keep him in perfect peace, whose mind is stayed on thee; because he trusteth in thee." - Isaiah 26:3

"Thou wilt keep him in perfect peace, whose mind is stayed on thee; because he trusteth in thee." - Isaiah 26:3

"Thou wilt keep him in perfect peace, whose mind is stayed on thee; because he trusteth in thee." - Isaiah 26:3

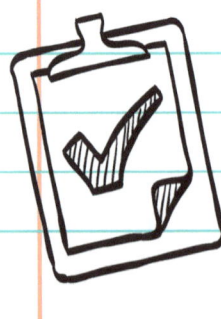

"Thou wilt keep him in perfect peace, whose mind is stayed on thee; because he trusteth in thee." - Isaiah 26:3

Visions

Goals

Milestones

Habits

Spiritual Reflection

Personal Reflection

SPIRITUAL WELLNESS IN TERMS OF THE SPIRIT

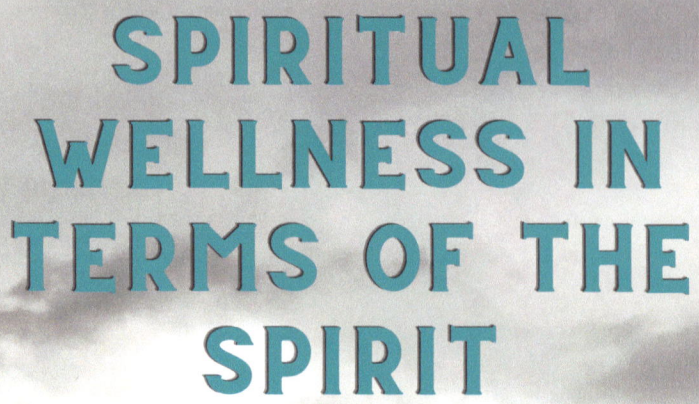

"If we live in the spirit, let us also walk in the spirit."

— Galatians 5:25

SECTION 1: CHAPTER 5
SPIRITUAL WELLNESS IN TERMS
OF THE SPIRIT

"If we live in the spirit, let us also walk in the spirit."

— Galatians 5:25

"If we live in the spirit, let us also walk in the spirit."

— Galatians 5:25

"If we live in the spirit, let us also walk in the spirit."

— Galatians 5:25

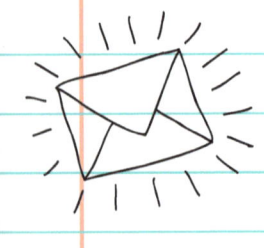

"If we live in the spirit, let us also walk in the spirit."

— Galatians 5:25

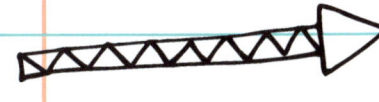

"If we live in the spirit, let us also walk in the spirit."

— Galatians 5:25

Visions

Goals

Milestones

Habits

Spiritual Reflection

Personal Reflection

TRUSTING IN GOD

"Trust in the Lord with all your heart and lean not on your own understanding. In all your ways acknowledge Him, and He will make your path straight". — Proverbs 3:5

SECTION 1: CHAPTER 6
TRUSTING IN GOD

"Trust in the Lord with all your heart and lean not on your own understanding. In all your ways acknowledge Him, and He will make your path straight". — Proverbs 3:5

YES!

"Trust in the Lord with all your heart and lean not on your own understanding. In all your ways acknowledge Him, and He will make your path straight". — Proverbs 3:5

"Trust in the Lord with all your heart and lean not on your own understanding. In all your ways acknowledge Him, and He will make your path straight". — Proverbs 3:5

"Trust in the Lord with all your heart and lean not on your own understanding. In all your ways acknowledge Him, and He will make your path straight". — Proverbs 3:5

"Trust in the Lord with all your heart and lean not on your own understanding. In all your ways acknowledge Him, and He will make your path straight". — Proverbs 3:5

Visions

Goals

Milestones

Habits

Spiritual Reflection

Personal Reflection

I Am More Than A Conqueror

SECTION 2:

THE BENEFITS OF SPIRITUAL WELLNESS

BENEFITS OF SPIRITUAL WELLNESS ON THE BODY

It is sown a natural body; it is raised a spiritual body. There is a natural body, and there is a spiritual body. — 1 Corinthian 15:44

SECTION 2: CHAPTER 1
BENEFITS OF SPIRITUAL WELLNESS ON THE BODY

It is sown a natural body; it is raised a spiritual body. There is a natural body, and there is a spiritual body. — 1 Corinthian 15:44

And we know that all things work together for the good of those who love God, to those who are the call according to his purpose. - Romans 8:28

And we know that all things work together for the good of those who love God, to those who are the call according to his purpose. - Romans 8:28

It is sown a natural body; it is raised a spiritual body. There is a natural body, and there is a spiritual body. — 1 Corinthian 15:44

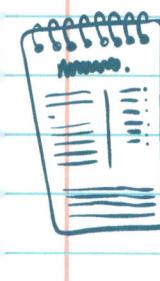

It is sown a natural body; it is raised a spiritual body. There is a natural body, and there is a spiritual body. — 1 Corinthian 15:44

Visions

Goals

Milestones

Habits

Spiritual Reflection

Personal Reflection

BENEFITS OF SPIRITUAL WELLNESS ON THE MIND

"Thou wilt keep in perfect peace, whose mind is stayed on thee: because he

trusteth in thee." — Isaiah 26:3

SECTION 2: CHAPTER 2
BENEFITS OF SPIRITUAL WELLNESS ON THE MIND

"Thou wilt keep in perfect peace, whose mind is stayed on thee: because he trusteth in thee." — Isaiah 26:3

"Thou wilt keep in perfect peace, whose mind is stayed on thee: because he trusteth in thee." — Isaiah 26:3

"Thou wilt keep in perfect peace, whose mind is stayed on thee: because he trusteth in thee." — Isaiah 26:3

"Thou wilt keep in perfect peace, whose mind is stayed on thee: because he trusteth in thee." — Isaiah 26:3

"Thou wilt keep in perfect peace, whose mind is stayed on thee: because he trusteth in thee." — Isaiah 26:3

Visions

Goals

Milestones

Habits

Spiritual Reflection

Personal Reflection

BENEFITS OF SPIRITUAL WELLNESS ON THE SPIRIT

"Now the Lord is that spirit: and where the spirit of the Lord is, there is liberty."

— 2 Corinthians 3:17

SECTION 2: CHAPTER 3
BENEFITS OF SPIRITUAL WELLNESS ON THE SPIRIT

"Now the Lord is that spirit: and where the spirit of the Lord is, there is liberty."

— 2 Corinthians 3:17

"Now the Lord is that spirit: and where the spirit of the Lord is, there is liberty."

— 2 Corinthians 3:17

"Now the Lord is that spirit: and where the spirit of the Lord is, there is liberty."

— 2 Corinthians 3:17

"Now the Lord is that spirit: and where the spirit of the Lord is, there is liberty."

— 2 Corinthians 3:17

"Now the Lord is that spirit: and where the spirit of the Lord is, there is liberty."

— 2 Corinthians 3:17

Visions

Goals

Milestones

Habits

Spiritual Reflection

Personal Reflection

BEHAVIOR FOLLOWS THOUGHT

"As a man thinketh in his heart, so is he."

— *Proverbs* 23:7

SECTION 2: CHAPTER 4
BEHAVIOR FOLLOWS THOUGHT

"As a man thinketh in his heart, so is he."

— Proverbs 23:7

"As a man thinketh in his heart, so is he."

— Proverbs 23:7

"As a man thinketh in his heart, so is he."

— Proverbs 23:7

"As a man thinketh in his heart, so is he."

— Proverbs 23:7

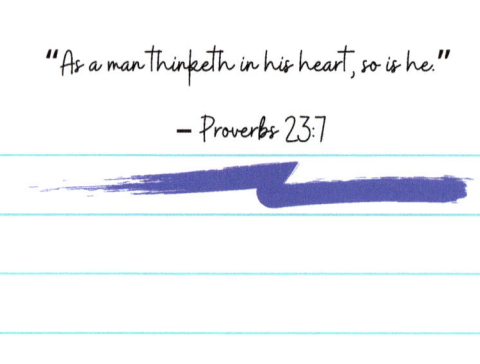

"As a man thinketh in his heart, so is he."

— Proverbs 23:7

Visions

Goals

Milestones

Habits

Spiritual Reflection

Personal Reflection

NEW REACTIONS TO OLD PATTERNS

"And no man putteth new wine into old bottles; else the new wine will burst the bottles, and be spilled, and the bottles shall perish." — Luke 5:37

SECTION 2: CHAPTER 5
NEW REACTIONS TO OLD PATTERNS

"And no man putteth new wine into old bottles; else the new wine will burst the bottles, and be spilled, and the bottles shall perish." — Luke 5:37

"And no man putteth new wine into old bottles; else the new wine will burst the bottles, and be spilled, and the bottles shall perish." — Luke 5:37

"And no man putteth new wine into old bottles; else the new wine will burst the bottles, and be spilled, and the bottles shall perish." — Luke 5:37

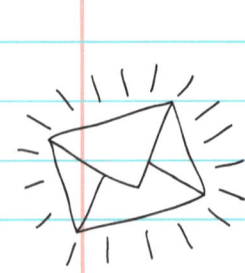

"And no man putteth new wine into old bottles; else the new wine will burst the bottles, and be spilled, and the bottles shall perish." — Luke 5:37

"And no man putteth new wine into old bottles; else the new wine will burst the bottles, and be spilled, and the bottles shall perish." — Luke 5:37

Visions

Goals

Milestones

Habits

Spiritual Reflection

Personal Reflection

A TRULY POSITIVE ATTITUDE FROM WITHIN

"I can do all things through Christ which strengtheneth me." — Philippians 4:13

— Proverbs 3:5

SECTION 2: CHAPTER 6
A TRULY POSITIVE ATTITUDE FROM WITHIN

"I can do all things through Christ which strengtheneth me." — Philippians 4:13

— Proverbs 3:5

yes!

"I can do all things through Christ which strengtheneth me." — Philippians 4:13

— Proverbs 3:5

"I can do all things through Christ which strengtheneth me." – Philippians 4:13

– Proverbs 3:5

"I can do all things through Christ which strengtheneth me." — Philippians 4:13

— Proverbs 3:5

"I can do all things through Christ which strengtheneth me." — Philippians 4:13

— Proverbs 3:5

Visions

Goals

Milestones

Habits

Spiritual Reflection

Personal Reflection

I Am Whole

SECTION 3:

DEVELOPING THE QUALITIES OF SPIRITUAL WELLNESS

GRACIOUSNESS

"For the grace of God that bringeth salvation has appeared to all men,"

— Titus 2:11

SECTION 3: CHAPTER 1

GRACIOUSNESS

"For the grace of God that bringeth salvation has appeared to all men,"

— Titus 2:11

"For the grace of God that bringeth salvation has appeared to all men,"

— Titus 2:11

"For the grace of God that bringeth salvation has appeared to all men,"

— Titus 2:11

"For the grace of God that bringeth salvation has appeared to all men,"

— Titus 2:11

"For the grace of God that bringeth salvation has appeared to all men,"

— Titus 2:11

Visions

Goals

Milestones

Habits

Spiritual Reflection

Personal Reflection

COMPASSION

"Finally, be ye all of one mind, having compassion one of another, love as brethren,

be pitiful, be courteous." — 1 Peter 3:8

SECTION 3: CHAPTER 2
COMPASSION

"Finally, be ye all of one mind, having compassion one of another, love as brethren,

be pitiful, be courteous." — 1 Peter 3:8

"Finally, be ye all of one mind, having compassion one of another, love as brethren, be pitiful, be courteous." — 1 Peter 3:8

"Finally, be ye all of one mind, having compassion one of another, love as brethren, be pitiful, be courteous." — 1 Peter 3:8

"Finally, be ye all of one mind, having compassion one of another, love as brethren, be pitiful, be courteous." — 1 Peter 3:8

"Finally, be ye all of one mind, having compassion one of another, love as brethren,

be pitiful, be courteous." — 1 Peter 3:8

Visions

Goals

Milestones

Habits

Spiritual Reflection

Personal Reflection

HIGH SELF-ESTEEM

"Let nothing be done through strife or vainglory; but in lowliness of mind let each esteem other better than themselves." — *Philippians 2:3*

SECTION 3: CHAPTER 3
HIGH SELF-ESTEEM

"Let nothing be done through strife or vainglory; but in lowliness of mind let each esteem other better than themselves." — Philippians 2:3

"Let nothing be done through strife or vainglory; but in lowliness of mind let each esteem other better than themselves." — Philippians 2:3

"Let nothing be done through strife or vainglory; but in lowliness of mind let each esteem other better than themselves." — Philippians 2:3

"Let nothing be done through strife or vainglory; but in lowliness of mind let each esteem other better than themselves." — Philippians 2:3

"Let nothing be done through strife or vainglory; but in lowliness of mind let each esteem other better than themselves." — Philippians 2:3

Visions

Goals

Milestones

Habits

Spiritual Reflection

Personal Reflection

HUMILITY

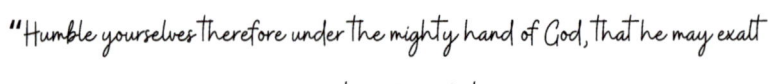

"Humble yourselves therefore under the mighty hand of God, that he may exalt you in due time." — 1 Peter 5:6

SECTION 3: CHAPTER 4
HUMILITY

"Humble yourselves therefore under the mighty hand of God, that he may exalt you in due time." — 1 Peter 5:6

"Humble yourselves therefore under the mighty hand of God, that he may exalt you in due time." — 1 Peter 5:6

"Humble yourselves therefore under the mighty hand of God, that he may exalt you in due time." — 1 Peter 5:6

"Humble yourselves therefore under the mighty hand of God, that he may exalt you in due time." — 1 Peter 5:6

"Humble yourselves therefore under the mighty hand of God, that he may exalt you in due time." — 1 Peter 5:6

Visions

Goals

Milestones

Habits

Spiritual Reflection

Personal Reflection

PATIENCE

"But let patience have her perfect work, that ye may be perfect and entire, wanting nothing." — James 1:4

SECTION 3: CHAPTER 5
PATIENCE

"But let patience have her perfect work, that ye may be perfect and entire, wanting nothing." — James 1:4

"But let patience have her perfect work, that ye may be perfect and entire, wanting nothing." – James 1:4

"But let patience have her perfect work, that ye may be perfect and entire, wanting nothing." — James 1:4

"But let patience have her perfect work, that ye may be perfect and entire, wanting nothing." — James 1:4

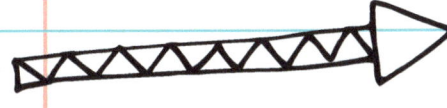

"But let patience have her perfect work, that ye may be perfect and entire, wanting nothing." — James 1:4

Visions

Goals

Milestones

Habits

Spiritual Reflection

Personal Reflection

HONESTY

"Finally, brethren, whatsoever things are true, whatsoever things are honorable, whatsoever things are just, whatsoever things are pure, whatsoever things are lovely, whatsoever things are of good report; if there be any virtue, and if there be any praise, think on these things."

— Philippians 4:8

SECTION 3: CHAPTER 6
HONESTY

"Finally, brethren, whatsoever things are true, whatsoever things are honorable, whatsoever things are just, whatsoever things are pure, whatsoever things are lovely, whatsoever things are of good report; if there be any virtue, and if there be any praise, think on these things."

— Philippians 4:8

yes!

"Finally, brethren, whatsoever things are true, whatsoever things are honorable, whatsoever things are just, whatsoever things are pure, whatsoever things are lovely, whatsoever things are of good report; if there be any virtue, and if there be any praise, think on these things." — Philippians 4:8

"Finally, brethren, whatsoever things are true, whatsoever things are honorable, whatsoever things are just, whatsoever things are pure, whatsoever things are lovely, whatsoever things are of good report; if there be any virtue, and if there be any praise, think on these things."

— Philippians 4:8

"Finally, brethren, whatsoever things are true, whatsoever things are honorable, whatsoever things are just, whatsoever things are pure, whatsoever things are lovely, whatsoever things are of good report; if there be any virtue, and if there be any praise, think on these things." — Philippians 4:8

"Finally, brethren, whatsoever things are true, whatsoever things are honorable, whatsoever things are just, whatsoever things are pure, whatsoever things are lovely, whatsoever things are of good report; if there be any virtue, and if there be any praise, think on these things." — Philippians 4:8

Visions

Goals

Milestones

Habits

Spiritual Reflection

Personal Reflection

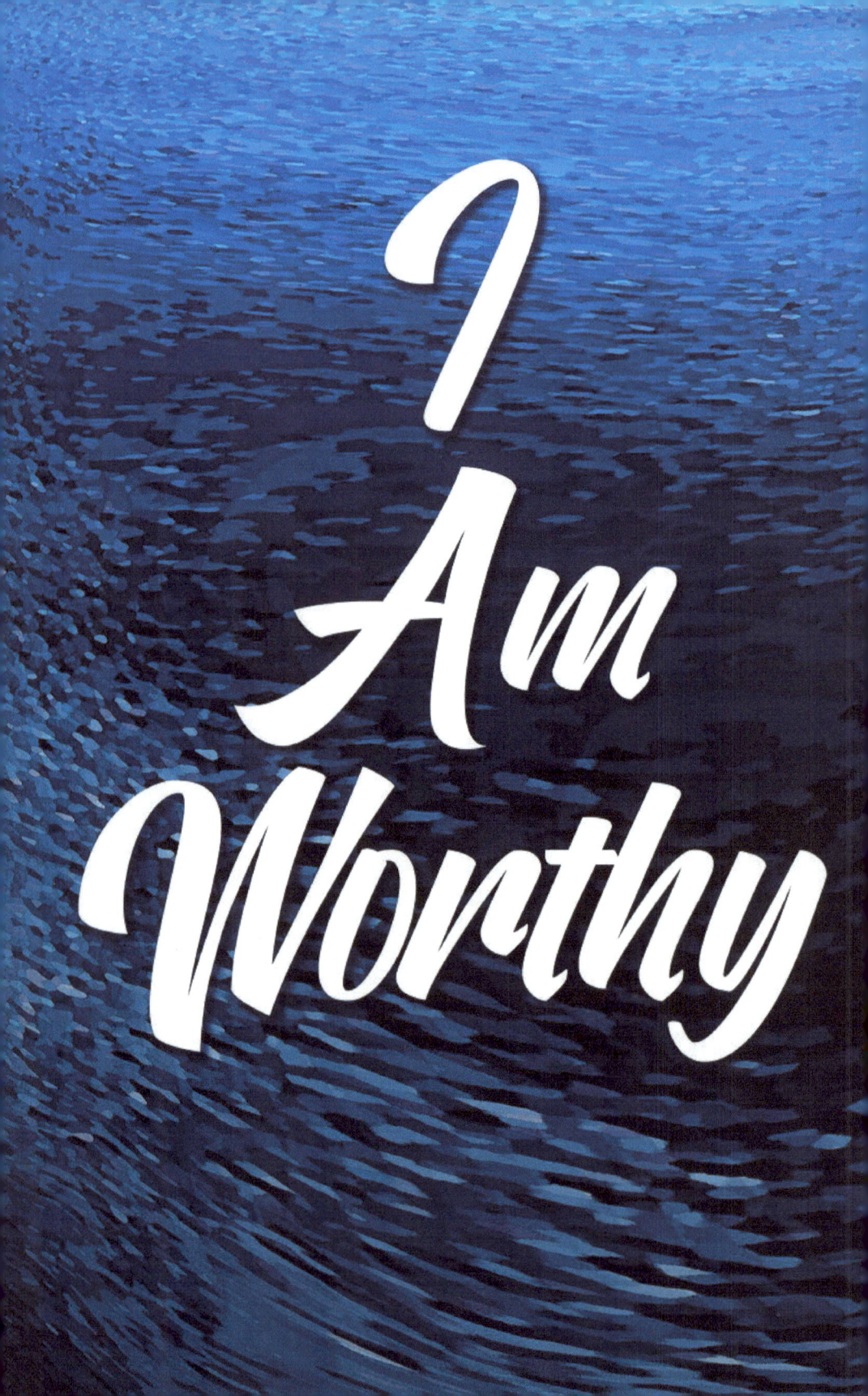

I Am Worthy

SECTION 4:

INTEGRATING SPIRITUAL WELLNESS INTO DAILY LIFE

ALIGNING YOUR VALUES, PRINCIPLES, MORALS, AND BELIEFS WITH YOUR LIFESTYLE

"In all things shewing thyself a pattern of good works: in doctrine shewing uncorruptness, gravity, sincerity, sound speech, that cannot be condemned; that he that is of the contrary part may be ashamed, having no evil things to say of you." – Titus 2:7-8

SECTION 4: CHAPTER 1
ALIGNING YOUR VALUES, PRINCIPLES, MORALS, AND BELIEFS WITH YOUR LIFESTYLE

"In all things shewing thyself a pattern of good works: in doctrine shewing uncorruptness, gravity, sincerity, sound speech, that cannot be condemned; that he that is of the contrary part may be ashamed, having no evil things to say of you." — Titus 2:7-8

"In all things shewing thyself a pattern of good works: in doctrine shewing uncorruptness, gravity, sincerity, sound speech, that cannot be condemned; that he that is of the contrary part may be ashamed, having no evil things to say of you." — Titus 2:7-8

"In all things shewing thyself a pattern of good works: in doctrine shewing uncorruptness, gravity, sincerity, sound speech, that cannot be condemned; that he that is of the contrary part may be ashamed, having no evil things to say of you." – Titus 2:7-8

"In all things shewing thyself a pattern of good works: in doctrine shewing uncorruptness, gravity, sincerity, sound speech, that cannot be condemned; that he that is of the contrary part may be ashamed, having no evil things to say of you." — Titus 2:7-8

"In all things shewing thyself a pattern of good works: in doctrine shewing uncorruptness, gravity, sincerity, sound speech, that cannot be condemned; that he that is of the contrary part may be ashamed, having no evil things to say of you." — Titus 2:7-8

Visions

Goals

Milestones

Habits

Spiritual Reflection

Personal Reflection

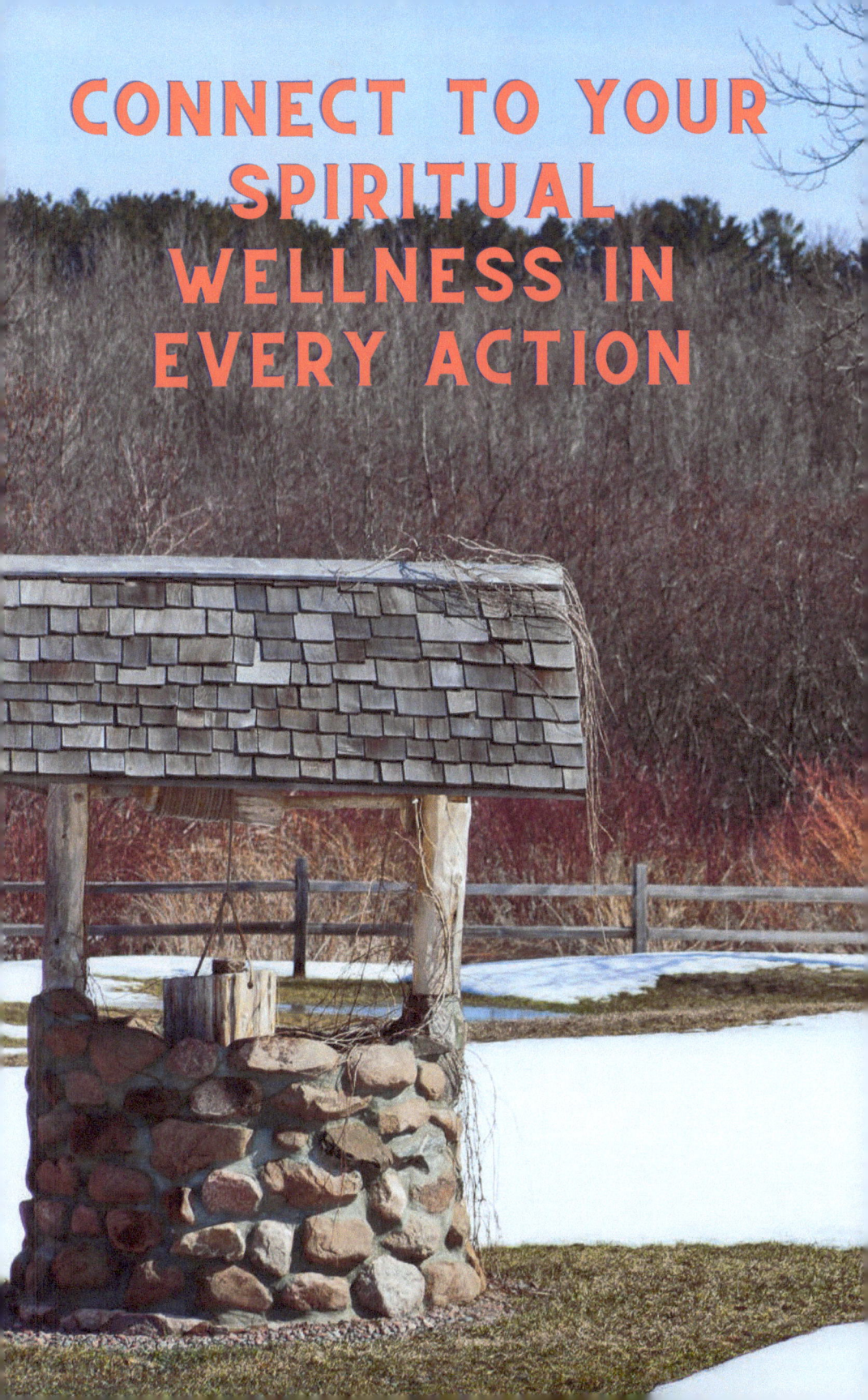

CONNECT TO YOUR SPIRITUAL WELLNESS IN EVERY ACTION

"In all thy ways, acknowledge him, and he shall direct thy tasks."

— Proverbs 3:6

SECTION 4: CHAPTER 2
CONNECT TO YOUR SPIRITUAL WELLNESS IN EVERY ACTION

"In all thy ways, acknowledge him, and he shall direct thy tasks."

— Proverbs 3:6

"In all thy ways, acknowledge him, and he shall direct thy tasks."

— Proverbs 3:6

"In all thy ways, acknowledge him, and he shall direct thy tasks."

— Proverbs 3:6

"In all thy ways, acknowledge him, and he shall direct thy tasks."

— Proverbs 3:6

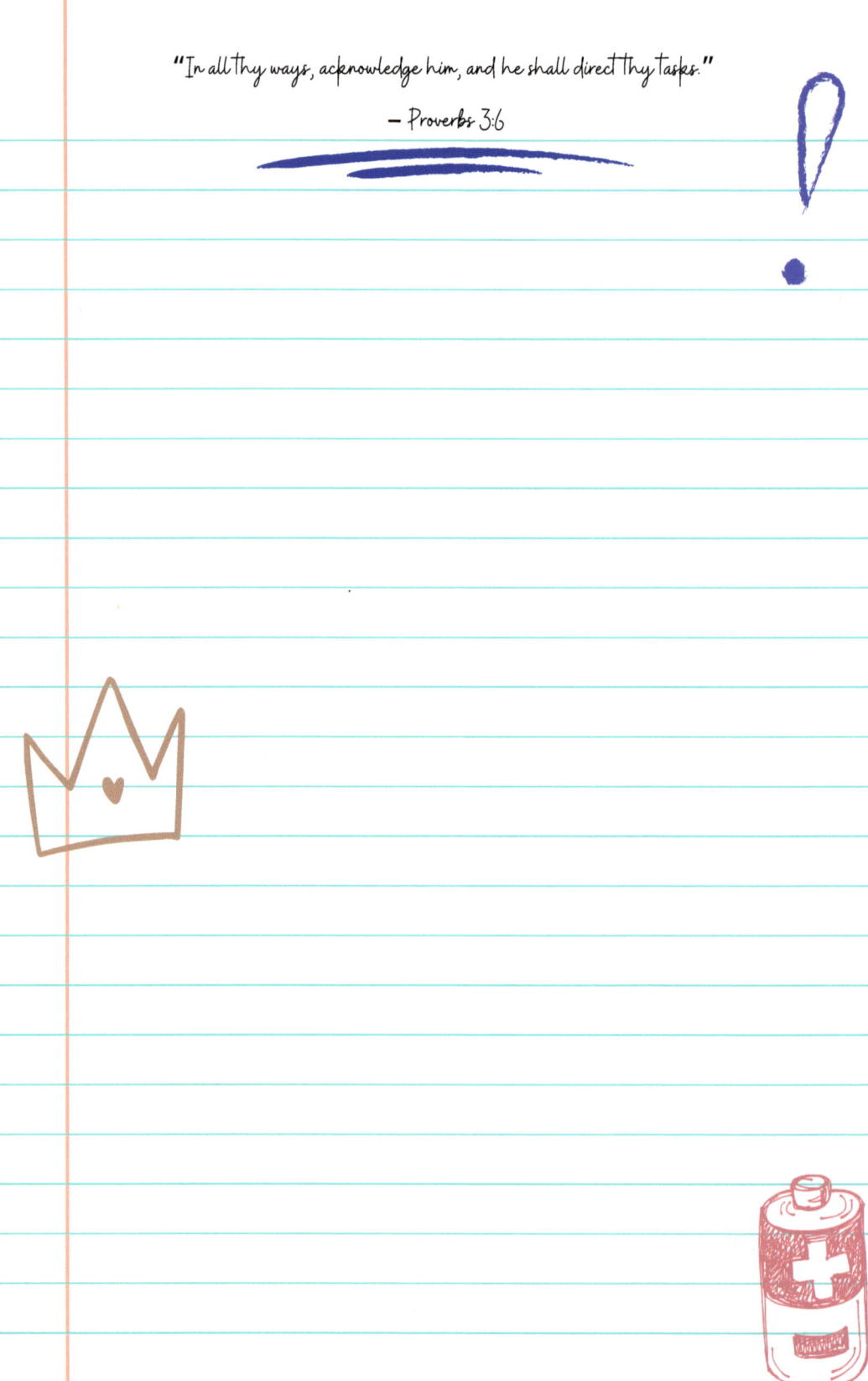

"In all thy ways, acknowledge him, and he shall direct thy tasks."

— Proverbs 3:6

Visions

Goals

Milestones

Habits

Spiritual Reflection

Personal Reflection

RELATING TO YOUR COMMUNITY AND THE WORLD

"And the Lord said unto the servant, go out into the highway and hedges, and compel them to come in, that my house may be filled." — Luke 14:23

SECTION 4: CHAPTER 3
RELATING TO YOUR COMMUNITY AND THE WORLD

"And the Lord said unto the servant, go out into the highway and hedges, and compel them to come in, that my house may be filled." — Luke 14:23

"And the Lord said unto the servant, go out into the highway and hedges, and compel them to come in, that my house may be filled." — Luke 14:23

"And the Lord said unto the servant, go out into the highway and hedges, and compel them to come in, that my house may be filled." — Luke 14:23

"And the Lord said unto the servant, go out into the highway and hedges, and compel them to come in, that my house may be filled." — Luke 14:23

"And the Lord said unto the servant, go out into the highway and hedges, and compel them to come in, that my house may be filled." — Luke 14:23

Visions

Goals

Milestones

Habits

Spiritual Reflection

Personal Reflection

USING SPIRITUAL WELLNESS TO MAKE DECISIONS

"Commit thy way unto the Lord; trust also in him; and he shall bring it to pass."

— Psalms 37:5

SECTION 4: CHAPTER 4
USING SPIRITUAL WELLNESS TO MAKE DECISIONS

"Commit thy way unto the Lord; trust also in him; and he shall bring it to pass."
— Psalms 37:5

"Commit thy way unto the Lord; trust also in him; and he shall bring it to pass."

— Psalms 37:5

"Commit thy way unto the Lord; trust also in him; and he shall bring it to pass."

— Psalms 37:5

"Commit thy way unto the Lord; trust also in him; and he shall bring it to pass."

— Psalms 37:5

"Commit thy way unto the Lord; trust also in him; and he shall bring it to pass."

— Psalms 37:5

Visions

Goals

Milestones

Habits

Spiritual Reflection

Personal Reflection

SPIRITUAL WELLNESS FOR GROUNDING AND RESILIENCE

"For to be carnally minded is death; but to be spiritually minded is life and peace."

— Romans 8:6

SECTION 4: CHAPTER 5
SPIRITUAL WELLNESS FOR GROUNDING AND RESILIENCE

"For to be carnally minded is death; but to be spiritually minded is life and peace."

— Romans 8:6

"For to be carnally minded is death; but to be spiritually minded is life and peace."

— Romans 8:6

"For to be carnally minded is death; but to be spiritually minded is life and peace."

— Romans 8:6

"For to be carnally minded is death; but to be spiritually minded is life and peace."

— Romans 8:6

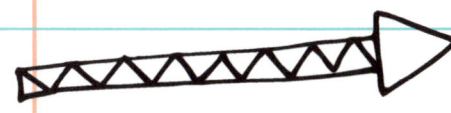

"For to be carnally minded is death; but to be spiritually minded is life and peace."

— Romans 8:6

Visions

Goals

Milestones

Habits

Spiritual Reflection

Personal Reflection

SPIRITUAL WELLNESS AND ITS EFFECT ON HEALTH

"And the prayer of faith shall save the sick, and the Lord shall raise him up; and if he have committed sins, they shall be forgiven him." — James 5:15

SECTION 4: CHAPTER 6
SPIRITUAL WELLNESS AND ITS EFFECT ON HEALTH

"And the prayer of faith shall save the sick, and the Lord shall raise him up; and if he have committed sins, they shall be forgiven him." – James 5:15

yes!

"And the prayer of faith shall save the sick, and the Lord shall raise him up; and if he have committed sins, they shall be forgiven him." — James 5:15

"And the prayer of faith shall save the sick, and the Lord shall raise him up; and if he have committed sins, they shall be forgiven him." — James 5:15

"And the prayer of faith shall save the sick, and the Lord shall raise him up; and if he have committed sins, they shall be forgiven him." — James 5:15

"And the prayer of faith shall save the sick, and the Lord shall raise him up; and if he have committed sins, they shall be forgiven him." — James 5:15

Visions

Goals

Milestones

Habits

Spiritual Reflection

Personal Reflection

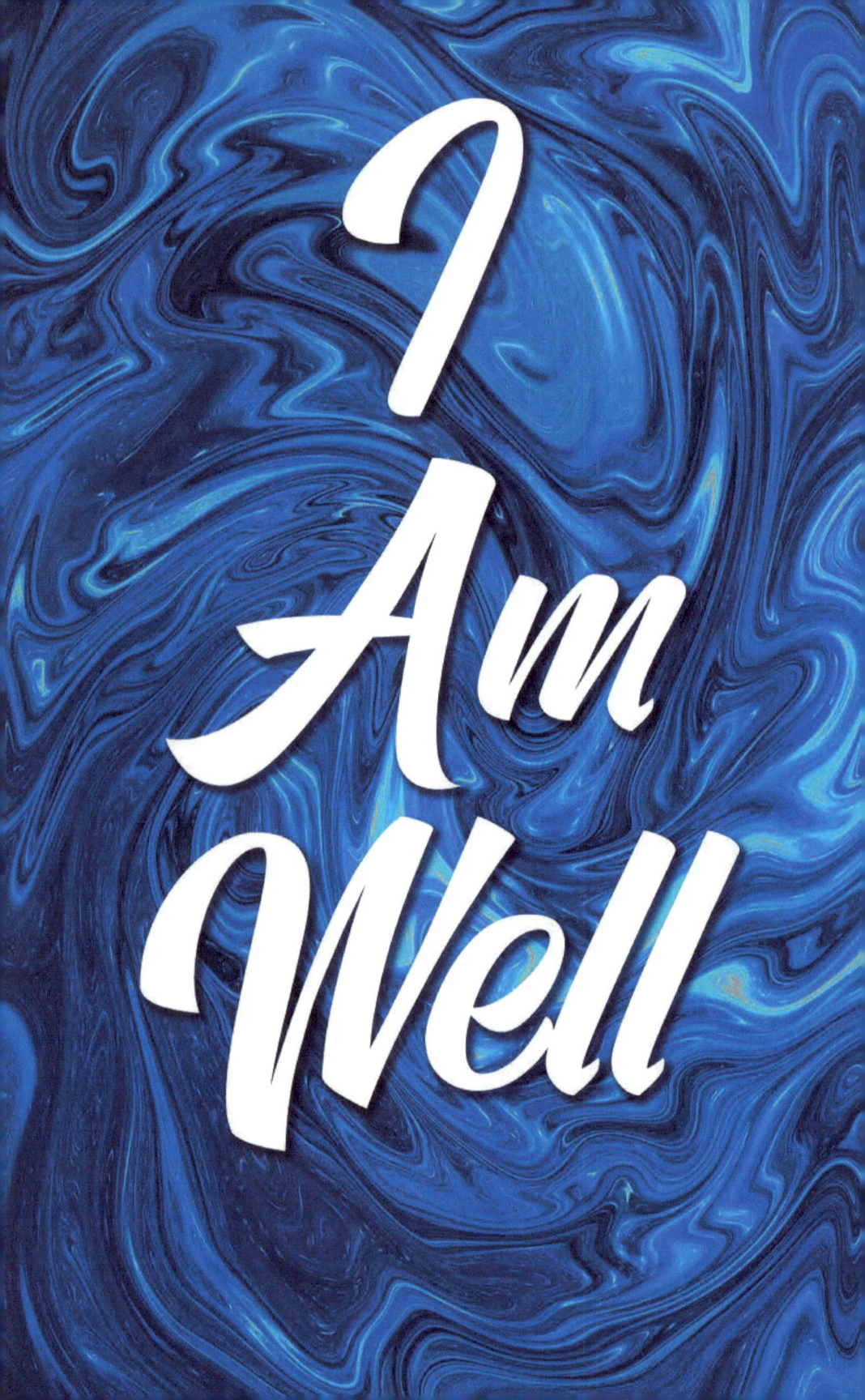

I Am Well

SECTION 5:

PRACTICES TO CULTIVATE SPIRITUAL WELLNESS

MEDITATION

"But his delight is in the law of the Lord; and in his law doth he meditate day and night." — Psalms 1:2

SECTION 5: CHAPTER 1
MEDITATION

"But his delight is in the law of the Lord; and in his law doth he meditate day and night." — Psalms 1:2

"But his delight is in the law of the Lord; and in his law doth he meditate day and night." — Psalms 1:2

"But his delight is in the law of the Lord; and in his law doth he meditate day and night." — Psalms 1:2

"But his delight is in the law of the Lord; and in his law doth he meditate day and night." — Psalms 1:2

"But his delight is in the law of the Lord; and in his law
doth he meditate day and night." — Psalms 1:2

Visions

Goals

Milestones

Habits

Spiritual Reflection

Personal Reflection

TIME IN NATURE

"When I consider thy heaven, the work of thy fingers, the moon and the stars, which thou hast ordained; what is man, that thou are mindful of him? And the son of man, that thou visitest him?" — Psalms 8:3-4

SECTION 5: CHAPTER 2

TIME IN NATURE

"When I consider thy heaven, the work of thy fingers, the moon and the stars, which thou hast ordained; what is man, that thou are mindful of him? And the son of man, that thou visitest him?" — Psalms 8:3-4

"When I consider thy heaven, the work of thy fingers, the moon and the stars, which thou hast ordained; what is man, that thou are mindful of him? And the son of man, that thou visitest him?" — Psalms 8:3-4

"When I consider thy heaven, the work of thy fingers, the moon and the stars, which thou hast ordained; what is man, that thou are mindful of him? And the son of man, that thou visitest him?" — Psalms 8:3-4

"When I consider thy heaven, the work of thy fingers, the moon and the stars, which thou hast ordained; what is man, that thou are mindful of him? And the son of man, that thou visitest him?" — Psalms 8:3-4

"When I consider thy heaven, the work of thy fingers, the moon and the stars, which thou hast ordained; what is man, that thou are mindful of him? And the son of man, that thou visitest him?" — Psalms 8:3-4

Visions

Goals

Milestones

Habits

Spiritual Reflection

Personal Reflection

PRAYER AND GRATITUDE

"Pray without ceasing."

— Thessalonians 5:17

SECTION 5: CHAPTER 3
PRAYER AND GRATITUDE

"Pray without ceasing."

— Thessalonians 5:17

"Pray without ceasing."

— Thessalonians 5:17

"Pray without ceasing."

— Thessalonians 5:17

"Pray without ceasing."

— Thessalonians 5:17

"Pray without ceasing."

— Thessalonians 5:17

Visions

Goals

Milestones

Habits

Spiritual Reflection

Personal Reflection

JOURNALING

"And the Lord answered me, and said, write the vision, and make it plain upon tables, that he may run that readeth it." — Habakkuk 2:2

SECTION 5: CHAPTER 4
JOURNALING

"And the Lord answered me, and said, write the vision, and make it plain upon tables, that he may run that readeth it." — Habakkuk 2:2

"And the Lord answered me, and said, write the vision, and make it plain upon tables, that he may run that readeth it." — Habakkuk 2:2

"And the Lord answered me, and said, write the vision, and make it plain upon tables, that he may run that readeth it." — Habakkuk 2:2

"And the Lord answered me, and said, write the vision, and make it plain upon tables, that he may run that readeth it." — Habakkuk 2:2

"And the Lord answered me, and said, write the vision, and make it plain upon tables, that he may run that readeth it." — Habakkuk 2:2

Visions

Goals

Milestones

Habits

Spiritual Reflection

Personal Reflection

READING & LISTENING

"Wherefore, my beloved brethren, let every man be swift to hear, slow to speak, slow to wrath." — James 1:19

SECTION 5: CHAPTER 5
READING AND LISTENING

"Wherefore, my beloved brethren, let every man be swift to hear, slow to speak, slow to wrath." — James 1:19

"Wherefore, my beloved brethren, let every man be swift to hear, slow to speak, slow to wrath." — James 1:19

"Wherefore, my beloved brethren, let every man be swift to hear, slow to speak, slow to wrath." — James 1:19

"Wherefore, my beloved brethren, let every man be swift to hear, slow to speak, slow to wrath." — James 1:19

"Wherefore, my beloved brethren, let every man be swift to hear, slow to speak, slow to wrath." — James 1:19

Visions

Goals

Milestones

Habits

Spiritual Reflection

Personal Reflection

PRAISE

"Let every thing that hath breath praise the Lord. Praise ye the Lord."

- Psalms 150:6

SECTION 5: CHAPTER 6
PRAISE

"Let every thing that hath breath praise the Lord. Praise ye the Lord."

- Psalms 150:6

Yes!

"Let every thing that hath breath praise the Lord. Praise ye the Lord."

- Psalms 150:6

"Let every thing that hath breath praise the Lord. Praise ye the Lord."

- Psalms 150:6

"Let every thing that hath breath praise the Lord. Praise ye the Lord."

- Psalms 150:6

"Let every thing that hath breath praise the Lord. Praise ye the Lord."

- Psalms 150:6

Visions

Goals

Milestones

Habits

Spiritual Reflection

Personal Reflection

FIND A FAITH OR PLACE OF WORSHIP THAT YOU RESONATE WITH

SECTION 6:

PRACTICES TO CULTIVATE SPIRITUAL WELLNESS

"One Lord, one faith, one baptism, one, God and father of all, who is above all, and through all, and in you all." Ephesians 4:5-6

SECTION 5: BONUS CHAPTER
FINDING A FAITH OR PLACE OF WORSHIP
THAT YOU RESONATE WITH

"One Lord, one faith, one baptism, one, God and father of all, who is above all, and through all, and in you all." Ephesians 4:5-6

"One Lord, one faith, one baptism, one, God and father of all, who is above all, and through all, and in you all." Ephesians 4:5-6

"One Lord, one faith, one baptism, one, God and father of all, who is above all, and through all, and in you all." Ephesians 4:5-6

"One Lord, one faith, one baptism, one, God and father of all, who is above all, and through all, and in you all." Ephesians 4:5-6

About the Author

Beatrix Marie Curry, MSN, APRN, PMHNP, BTh is the author of Nurse Boss Nurse Boss: A Journey Through the Dark and Co-author of several author books. She is a trailblazer when it comes to wholeness and health on every level. Born and raised in Newark, New Jersey, she endured various struggles and triumphs in her life, which have helped to shape and mold the phenomenal woman you see today. Beatrix was catapulted into adulthood at the age of 16 after her beloved mother passed away in 1996.

Having experienced periods of depression in her life, she fights to raise awareness to this unspoken condition to help others achieve the freedom in God that she has been able to attain. Her dedication to mental health led her to become a Psychiatric Mental Health Nurse

Practitioner (PMHNP), transforming her own experiences with grief and depression into a source of strength to support others facing similar challenges. In addition to her extensive healthcare background, Beatrix holds a Bachelor's degree in Theology, reinforcing her commitment to spiritual wellness and faith- based healing.

She has claimed the victory in making the best of all that God has given her in this life. This Woman of God has no qualms testifying how God Himself has surely given her beauty for her ashes. Beatrix walks in her calling as an Ordained Minister, Prophetess, Serial Entrepreneur, Healthcare Professional, Spiritual Wellness Coach, Mentor and Prophetic Intercessor. Her greatest desire is to relentlessly help anyone she can become the best version of themselves.

Beatrix has made it her life mission to aid others in achieving exceptional wellness encompassing a sound mind, a healthy body, and a right spirit. Regardless of the trial, Beatrix unceasingly exercises her faith in God time after time, and she genuinely desires to be an inspiration to show others how to do the same in their lives.

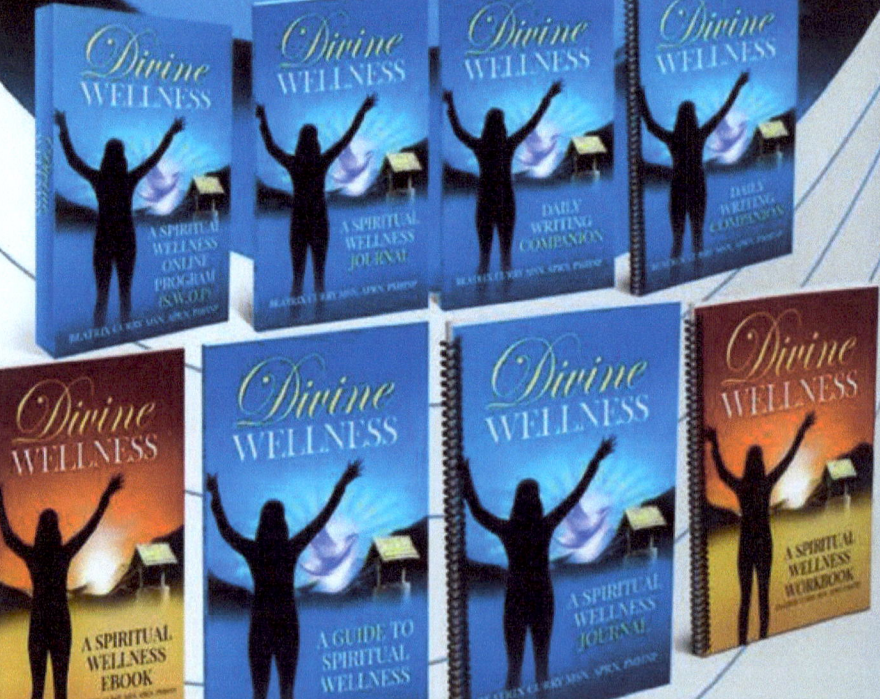

BEATRIX CURRY MSN, APRN, PMHNP
PRESENTS

Divine
WELLNESS
A GUIDE TO SPIRITUAL WELLNESS

AVAILABLE ONLINE & ON AMAZON

 BEATRIXCURRY@GMAIL.COM

WWW.DIVINEWELLNESSBOOKS.COM

For more information on how you can work with me, you can receive more information at:

http://www.divinewellnessbooks.com

beatrixcurry@gmail.com